The Definition of Empty

Mary Burritt
Christiansen
Poetry Series

Mary Burritt Christiansen Poetry Series
Hilda Raz, Series Editor

The Mary Burritt Christiansen Poetry Series publishes two to four books a year that engage and give voice to the realities of living, working, and experiencing the West and the Border as places and as metaphors. The purpose of the series is to expand access to, and the audience for, quality poetry, both single volumes and anthologies, that can be used for general reading as well as in classrooms.

Also available in the Mary Burritt Christiansen Poetry Series:

Ancestral Demon of a Grieving Bride: Poems by Sy Hoahwah
Feel Puma: Poems by Ray Gonzalez
Grief Land: Poems by Carrie Shipers
The Shadowgraph: Poems by James Cihlar
Crosscut: Poems by Sean Prentiss
The Music of Her Rivers: Poems by Renny Golden
to cleave: poems by Barbara Rockman
After Party: Poems by Noah Blaustein
The News as Usual: Poems by Jon Kelly Yenser
The Handyman's Guide to End Times: Poems by Juan J. Morales

For additional titles in the Mary Burritt Christiansen Poetry Series, please visit unmpress.com.

THE DEFINITION OF
EMPTY

poems

BILL O'NEILL

University of New Mexico Press | Albuquerque

Library of Congress Cataloging-in-Publication Data
Names: O'Neill, Bill (William Baldwin), author.
Title: The definition of empty: poems / Bill O'Neill.
Other titles: Mary Burritt Christiansen poetry series.
Description: Albuquerque: University of New Mexico Press, 2021. |
    Series: Mary Burritt Christiansen poetry series
Identifiers: LCCN 2020040357 (print) | LCCN 2020040358 (e-book) |
    ISBN 9780826362230 (paperback) | ISBN 9780826362247 (e-book)
Subjects: LCGFT: Poetry.
Classification: LCC PS3615.N436 D44 2021 (print) | LCC PS3615.N436 (e-book) |
    DDC 813.6—dc23
LC record available at https://lccn.loc.gov/2020040357
LC e-book record available at https://lccn.loc.gov/2020040358

Cover illustration by Felicia Cedillos
Designed by Felicia Cedillos
Composed in Meridien LT Std 10/14

Contents

Disclaimer

This book is a work of poetry. Names, characters, places, and incidents either are products of the author's imagination or are used fictitiously. Any resemblance to actual events or locales or persons, living or dead, is entirely coincidental.

Author's Note

This book is also dedicated to the youth who appeared before me in my role as executive director of the New Mexico Juvenile Parole Board. My poems about these youths reflect my own personal experience about their situations and are in no way an attempt to speak for them. The poems are, however, also meant to be a tribute to them and an acknowledgment of the many challenges they face.

I often tell others that the three years I had the privilege to work with incarcerated juveniles "changed my life." I say that because it is true. Of course, there are many other poems in *The Definition of Empty* that touch on other aspects of my life at the time.

I would also like to thank UNM Press for their patience and support with this manuscript—specifically Elise McHugh and Hilda Raz. I am truly honored to be published by this fine university press.

Bill O'Neill
Albuquerque, New Mexico
October 19, 2020

Cody

He is alone before us, as they always are,
at the long table,
only this time all rural with his working
cowboy relatives—bandanas, newly shined boots,
jeans—the whole lot of them shy &
polite, as they line the room,
as they await our decision.

"Cody," our chairwoman begins, "do you ever think about Jarrel?"

Cody's eyes moisten. "If you only knew, ma'am . . .
I think about him every day. He was my best friend. I
wish he could be here instead of me."

Now I remember the details: the newspaper headlines,
the tragedy, our own thick file
chronicling the keg party.

Teens on spring break.

Way out by the Texas line, in *that* part of the state.

Cody behind the wheel trying to impress, going too fast
in the middle of the field when suddenly everything
goes wrong, somersaulted into a silent finality,

a jarring rebuke of limitless youth.

"Can I read my letter now?" Cody asks, and
our chairwoman nods. "I am *so* sorry . . ." he begins.

And then I fade out as there is some memory of

mine

1

that wants to emerge, that wants its moment with me . . .
Yes, there I was, Cody's age, barreling in my dad's
borrowed Toronado, loaded down with all of my friends,
Friday night, across the tracks despite the flashing red lights
& suddenly the rumbling tonnage of reality is
right there, its light so high above us, & I gun it as
we narrowly miss our own public tragedy.

The back seat is silent now.

"What?" I protest. "It wasn't *that* close."

"Take me home now," I remember Sheila saying, quietly
placing her empty beer bottle back into the plastic covering.

Meanwhile, Cody is nearly finished with his pained reading
of what he would tell his dead friend when it starts to well
up, my own emotion public now. "Cody," I begin unsteadily,
"we believe you. No one in this room doubts the
sincerity of your remorse."

At this Cody's men join in communal grief; someone
passes the tissue box around.

"Thank you for coming. . . ." I add to no one specifically
in the jammed room, while I stamp his papers

with our approval.

Kimberly

"I don't want to see the disappointment in
their faces anymore," she says, her eyebrows
stitched together, her nose a sharp point.

"And then there is the pressure of being high,"
she continues. "Always having to stay high . . ."

Her elfin quality should have deterred the husband
of her mother's best friend from doing anything, let
alone what he did.

This particular day she is high before us on three
different alchemical wonders, administered of
course by our degreed doctor bartenders.

Riding the bus all day, across the river & back,
she had time to think about who exactly her father
was, & he is in her mind's eye a combination of three
different men—there, on her imaginary stage—informed
of course
by what is absent in her own life.

Down that street, that one night, when she did ninety

without a reason to stop.

Dagmar I

I have a friend who says things like: "You
know what I like about you? Everything I say
impresses you."

The power of speech in the morning—at the café,
or in the important gathering of juvenile justice professionals.

The ability to walk down an asphalt road, or the way
I can still hear Dagmar's stinging admonition of me
"not becoming a ghost in your own life."

Even the casualty of the noted lost decades—a J.
Crew catalogue of what was not right—this too a
miracle in its own way. This is what happens

when absence takes over.

Dagmar II

I have a friend who says things like: "You
should have read the suicide note. . . ."

Trying to get your attention, shock as a form of
truth.

And later, as we discuss the blessing of anonymous
cyber-dating: "It's just not an honest entry into
someone's world."

And then her eyes, almost black in their intensity,
discouraging my own animated ways:
"As long as you promise not to read me another one of *those*,"
she says, pointing to my accumulating stack of
accusation there on the bar. "We are in a public
place," she adds. "Don't yell at me."

"*Yell*?" I whisper incredulously.

"I work hard all day," she continues. "I am not
on the clock now. I have had a whole day of raw emotion.
So, unless you are willing to pay me, I
don't want to hear about it."

And yet, I point out to her, you complain about *his*
unwillingness to talk about his feelings, him being your
boyfriend.

"Okay," she allows, always looking away as she
does, rarely meeting my eyes. "Duly noted."

So, at this point, I continue to go deeper into the dictates
of solitary passion, as routines can always be refined,
or practiced infinitely, until you hear the deeper,
stranger
messages.

"*Look*," she says, resolute in her interruption, and
with finality:

"Stand outside of your tradition. Just once."

Indian Hospital

Today, she is euphoric, having missed the menacing
corner of her computer table.

"It could have been much worse," she says, taking
my arm as I lead her from work. "I mean, when I
fall, I am always aware of my *head*."

We walk through the silent hospital hallway, quiet
& neutral in its watching,

the chief's profile inlaid onto the floor.

"Anyway," she continues, as she gracefully
crabwalks down the frightening stairway, "that
chair was of no help. With its rollers . . ."

She is safely on earth now, & reenacts
her near catastrophe for my benefit, while
all I can think of is how great to see her
smile, all upbeat & excited, no matter
the cold implications of her Friday morning
triumph.

Her curly hair, her freckles—how lucky is
her trouble as we *finally* reach each other
across the decades, in our impossible truth . . .

the highlight of any conceivable day.

Hitch-Hiking at 28

The sun was my compass, the gallon
of water keeping me grounded on the road-
side, an unintended anchor.

I would extend my cardboard sign with each passing
car, an offering in exchange for direction,
& if fortunate could land in the back of a pickup
with its freedom from all conversational duties.

Pasco? Lewiston?

Waiting for sundown so that I could find a
place for my pad & red puffy bag, squared off
there in the freight yard or equivalent, making
it through another night unnoticed, & with
the arrival of yet another
dazzling
morning—this time the undulating dry hills
of the winding highway, Palouse Country—
the strong belief,

especially then,

that I was walking into anything I wanted.

Dagmar III

I have a friend who says things like: "I
don't need the barrier of your emotion
just to get to my job."

We are there, in the bar. She is drinking
something tall & exotic & green,
looking smart in her vintage coat and
her short, jet-black hair.

"If someone could just suck the raw
emotion out of my workplace . . ." she
continues wistfully, now asking for more
ginger sauce in between her plea for
universal truth.

"They do get worked up about the Harleys. I
have a cop there when I render those decisions."

Dagmar too is exploring the mystery of state
power—the life of a district attorney—as I
reach for the check, my government ID there
on the bar like a forgotten tip,

fifteen months into my sentence.

Cruzita

Please stop injecting yourself like that, I
want to say at some appropriate time during
the hearing. There is no reason to continue such
behavior, *on that level*, only the cries of
your own dreams, a bad mountain like what
awaits you on the outside, as we talk about
heroin, meth & crack, the characteristics of each.

"What will you do on the outs?" I ask. "Tell
them all to go away?"

Starting with your own tenuous mother &
her documented four DWIs. What a fierce need
or thirst for oblivion, poly-substance in its fullest
sense, and here she is in the unit: sixteen years old
with her acne & prison-issue & wanting only to
work on her levulls.

Do not let them muscle you like that, take over
your being with their solemn promising of wild
that only unlocks you into a habit characterized by

momentum.

A Quieter Heart

I do not know anything about the natural
world, it being largely off my radar screen &
irrelevant in my atmosphere of the dark
masculine twist—ridicule in the willing heart—
as across four lanes of traffic there *he*
is, Maximus. Untroubled, behind the wheel
of his flashy black SUV, never growing weary of
his own tactical soul, no danger of solemn
reflection, always drawing upon the account
of an unending self-interest,

the private joke that we men understand.

And so, I learn again how a brief glance can inhabit
the rest of the day. My dad's lessons of absence &
you are on your own buddy—but these guys like
Maximus will always be miles ahead of me
with these same lessons,

calculating their next move.

As right and universal as a five-year business plan,
& laughter around the pool table, closing-time approaching . . .

Off into the bachelor night. Something *other* than this
waiting to be coaxed out, needing only

perhaps

the memory of junior high science class—the window
open to April—the approaching noon of softball, and recess.

I had a quieter heart back then. Unformed.

The other stuff could have waited—murky adulthood—as
it has always been there, in the parking lot, adding
up to its own imperfection.

Like the view from Nine Mile Hill,
the city lights just there like a fact, belonging
to this metropolis that she blames me for
without hesitation.

The baseball lights have now been dimmed, &
somehow there can be a blend of cruelty and light—
talking, a clean & unambiguous handshake . . .

Belonging in the lineup as I do,
in spite of myself.

My Sabbatical

That summer was so promising . . . The interstate
through Wyoming, American flag on top of the desolate
crag, Laramie blooming like a stunted paradise.

Roadside hot springs, the seductive freights
relentless in their pounding, the nocturnal parking lot
outside—the cheap motel room with its uncertain
door—so many ideas for future incarnations.

The whole world to myself . . .

nothing but memory to keep me stable.

Castillo

A burned car, a gang named Valley Gardens,
the daily bong hit & more,
pants always necking below the waist,
which leads back to a circumstance & a striving
less lofty, grounded in limitation & the
causality of personal history.

Castillo tries to explain to us what he wants
from his life:

"I know my life can be better than this," he mutters,
tears welling up, his massive torso hunched
in the chair. "I know it can . . ."

And we know that too, having read his very thick
file: molested by his uncle, mother dazed &
absent on crack, biological father not really in
Heaven but in Medium Restrict. Seventeen,
the specifics of why he was shot no big deal as
the bullet only grazed his waist. He is a big
young man struggling through several medications
intended to erase what has come his way.

"Well, child," one of us begins, "where can
we send you? Where can you go? Realistically?"

His eyes brighten slightly, from the part of him
that is not sedated. "My Auntie. She lives in the Heights.
Has a job and stuff. She's all respectable. She wants
to give me a chance."

At this point I want to believe that in any sad story there
is an unvisited life that can take hold in its full glowing
form, & that Castillo speaks for all of us. It is always
like this, the same equation for these boys of
the reform school, as they appear before
us in this formal room with its strange carpeted walls.

And now, in that moment of collision between
intention & bad personal history, Castillo adds
quietly: "Sir, I *have* to believe that there is
something else . . . I have to."

Easter Weekend

Let us consider his hulking, overalled presence—
brown hairy neck an oak tree trunk—
& in his hand the last-minute Easter purchases,
before me at the Walgreen's, even the cashier
smiles when it is his turn.

As for me, I exit the parking lot & head north
into the languid afternoon,
up the street, returning home to no one, ready
to celebrate what I have chosen not to do with my life.

Easter baskets, the relentless succession of holidays
to be ignored, increasing reminders of how unusual
I am. The endless company of myself, & the
television that helps you welcome the night, stars
moving farther & farther away in their bright orbit.

Then, the Monday alarm trumpets your surrender
to the approved rhythms of *everyone else*, as
the workweek has begun, & by eleven that same
morning you are ready to resign

or at least go to some hiding place.

Still, it is important work, & maybe atonement
for the bankrolled years of searching
and well-intentioned flight.

Now you brave the captain's bridge high up on
the sailboat mast, your *other life* in the vast
ocean before you, as you call out orders to
the dubious crew,

the amnesia that comes with any titled position.

Joey

Little boy with brand-new sneakers, pressed
baggy pants & always less juvenile than we
imagine, bespectacled and earnest about his future,
this kid who five programs have rejected.

But the ex-boyfriend *stepfather* surfaces like
a good memory, willing to take him in, to
his own quarters next to the Ruidoso Stables. Joey's
dazed biological mother sits at the long table
in all of her apology; the stepfather's girlfriend
is there too—uncertain about all of this, but masking
it well—her gray hair parted in the middle as
they did in the sixties.

Joey wants us to read his notebook: rap lyrics,
poems, penciled drawings.

"I take ownership of the poems more, sir," he says
with his Sureños accent. "Because they are from my
heart."

He cannot resist reading one of them, about his
mother, who then tears up about the past in all of
its absence & degradation.

Hector the stepfather intercedes: "We are going to
make a cowboy out of this young man."

Today we love rural truth, or that pocket of
red so insistent, bitter & maddening.

"I have changed, Miss," Joey adds. "I am no longer so
gangsterous."

Everything then becomes Sunday-morning Mass
as smiling we grant him his freedom,
his tennis shoes giving way to cowboy boots, off
into the uncertain noon he will now go, hoping
for a break with his sketched drawings of Jesus
as his new family heads off into the spectacular
present that will not necessarily explode
into itself before they hit Lovington.

The Governor's Son

And finally, speaking of tenuous, the governor's
son is going to fly us away in a single-engine
plane that he jokes he has never flown before.
Predictably we hit something, taking off
from the roof, & it is a long way down, but

I never fared so well down there anyway.

Juan

And the other kid, a teenage Jack Webb through
his history of meth—California surfacing—
the flowering of his robberies along the beach,
and the odd pattern of missing golf carts.

He wants to be a radiologist. Or a Marine. As
with Joey he is different now too,
old-school in his manner.

"No more violence," he tells us softly. "Or robbingggs."

Juan knows the score, the divided opinions that preceded
his entrance into our silent hearing room; the long
table with its gallery of psychiatrists, teachers & state
officials.

He is perhaps thrown off by all of this attention, but
settles into a polite, formal delivery—poker-faced. One
of us asks if he is on medication.

"Just Seroquel, miss," he replies.

We help him out by explaining our theory
of Juan, & his countenance becomes even smoother,
like the ocean swells he and his fellow surfers
would quietly celebrate.

Unassailable he remains in his courtesy; our targeted
questions ring hollow until we finally submit.

"All right. It is a *yes*. Do you have any questions?"

He is silent, awkward in the good news.
"No, Miss. It just sounds so good . . ."

Quiet waves, maybe, with their calming sound at
midnight.

Monday Morning

She pulls my arm tighter, her grip one of flowering
desperation, the kind that will not give up.

"I did not fall today," she says cheerfully, proud
of what that means. "Good," I reply, monitoring her
enthusiasm.

There are bad logarithms, relentless in their
truth, but I will protect her as best I can.
We have shared the desert years, & they are
resplendent in our memory. Her grip nearly
tells our story, the firm clenching maybe not from
the standard need but it is what we have.

She knows that I will be her last uneasy guardian
if that is what is called for, and we flourish
in our early-morning routine. Today it is the
challenge of getting her to work, which means
getting her to my car, & through the parking lot,
& my God the stairs.

There is narrative in her grip, and maybe
one day she will paint it.

A Heart-to-Heart with Dad

"He will always be the secret master of my blood"
—STANLEY KUNITZ

The mountain hike with my eighty-five-year-old father,
where calculated as always he brings along a pocketknife—
his ancient but determined gait, up the rocky mountainside
into the high Idaho air we go.

He needs to stop, & I pretend to be winded as well, by now
a middle-aged boy too clear on this minuet, both
of us following and disavowing the obvious script. Our
attempt at reconciliation—my years of absence, I am *Biff*—
& even in his disappointment he has a curiosity, a desire
to somehow push into my inaccessible life.

"So," he begins, "do you have any kids anywhere? At
least that you know about?"

"No," I reply, pretending not to be stunned at this question.

Swiftly he moves on to the next topic, deftly
concealing his literal being from this relentlessly
confusing son.

His question continues to sting more than the sudden change
in altitude, though I suppose I can play this game up
to a point, which is the problem. It might have been different,
it *would* have been different, minus
the gift of Ohio silos & knowledge that came from
loitering among the farm-boys, raising themselves
too, united in our inevitable discoveries.

My father carves our initials into the rusting chairlift
pylon, & we share the view together. "Yeah, we made
it . . ." We echo each other with honest accomplishment, as
neither one of us wants to stare back
into those decades anyway.

Still, I know that *deep down* he would not have
had it gone this route.

Instead,

he would have left his teenage son a neatly
handwritten note, next to lit candles maybe,
with the assurance that there was indeed an opposite life
awaiting, all radiant & welcoming—despite the years
of *his* absence and harshness—as these intimate
candles would clearly indicate. He would have imparted
his wisdom like a well-meaning uncle, or a random
passenger next to you on a train.

He would have pointed me in a softer direction.

Marcello

His manner is dull, blunted as through
several medications he weighs whether or not
he can trust me.

"It was the first time we were down that street,"
Marcello begins, "I swear. We did not kill his cat."

I know, I know. . . . But why the medieval axe? It
was just there, in your friend's car?

"It was in the window. I just grabbed it."

So it was ornamental? But you put a gash in
your accuser's skull—

"Just seven stitches. He was beating up my friend."

Here we shift.

Is this place working for you? I mean, this
particular cottage? You are on medication, right?

"Just Lithium."

I don't mean to pry, but these random details help me to
remember your case. So, you like the Insane Clown Posse?

Marcello hesitates on this one, once again the balancing.
"Why do you ask me that?"

Because they are quite a band.

"Look," he continues, "a lot of things have happened
to me. I have these dark thoughts. Their music calms
me . . . makes me *like* this world."

And here I remember the hanging & the
cutting, how they taught him tennis at the Arizona
middle school.

Okay fellah, I say, just try to keep out of fights? We will
give you a positive report as I have not officially
heard anything to the contrary.

We will talk again in a couple of months.

Barabbas

There are these energies that pull us down,
that dictate the sum of ancient grievances
which will never fade as apology is only
hesitation.

She goes round & round, incredulous
at what actually transpired, and no one, she
feels, will actually *listen* to her.

I know that I would rather be elsewhere.

Zoning out, perhaps, on the florid, overdone
color tones of the Easter Week Movies: *Barabbas,*
The King of Kings, The Ten Commandments . . .

How warm they make me feel inside, well past
my usual bedtime hour, with their solemnity
of speech & fitting attention to the larger issues.
Yul Brynner to the edge of histrionic in front
of his queen, Anne Baxter, the dignity of his gestures
almost upstaging her withering commentary on his
masculine value.

And how can I *not* watch the *entirety* of Anthony
Quinn's grunting struggle of faith—all numb &
euphoric, alone in my warm bed—he enduring the
mine collapse & the shoveling of mud & even harnessed
like a horse in front of the plow with his other
Roman slave friend,

all on our behalf,

for decades, as he *cannot* violate himself
despite the choking degradation all around him,
mute intelligence carrying the day, or
at least until he sees the proof he needs
in the fires of Rome.

I want to include all of this in our morning
drive to work, but there is no room in our heated
silence for such an exchange. Instead,
it is all about being drenched in what was not
given,

& the impossibility of forgetting.

Marcos

"Game Over" on his two eyelids, inked in a
thinner line, thinner than the magic-marker-
sized letters "LOVE HATE" above his eyebrows,
his chances maybe in the distance between the
two.

He hesitates to sign the document, despite our
encouragement. "I don't know, sir. . . ." he shrugs,
speaking softly, grinning. "I am being set up
for failure," his use of this phrase strangely
coached. "They don't want me in their program.
They've told me as much. I just want to go home. . . ."

But there is no home, Marcos, I try to say
as diplomatically as possible, trying not to be
distracted by his shrugging &
joking,
a soft-boy gangster. Marcos has got *imagery*,
the caseworker had told us before the hearing.
Nobody ever cared about this kid. What is this, his
third commitment?

He is soon to be eighteen and will soon graduate
into you-know-what. His caseworker is also his translator
between our worlds, breaking it down
for him as he must have done earlier, when
they were alone in his solitary pod. He is good,
the caseworker, with his muscular black forearms
& pink Izod shirt. "Sign it, Marcos," his advocate
says, pulling him aside. "Then you will have a choice?
Don't sign and it is off the table—"

Peering into the future, as if. A poster boy
for *suicidal ideation*, which is a term buried
in his Bible-sized file. What do we say to a young man like
this? His fantastic circumstance of relatives un-imprisoned,
& how the dark energies are always with us,

reminding us of what we cannot believe.

Nonprofit Work

And now, realizing that I walked these streets
for others, always chasing the eye contact &
hope for the less fortunate.

Inevitably, the churches—with their oddly distracted
priests & ministers, begrudging us two minutes
from their stone lecterns—the cause delineated &
the pitch made, at all three exits we await, our
convicts dressed up and determined to show
the logic behind their losing. And at the county
fairs too, *everyone* in a good mood.

This for me when a full day could be believed,
raffle currency like affirmation in our hands,
preying upon the uncertain churchgoers, the
lengths we would go.

Every service, every Mass, every weekend.

And the inescapable conversation that filled the rest
of the week, donor prospects suspicious of my
sudden attention, until the urge to talk about themselves
takes over.

All of this justified, important, raw.

Tonight the opium syrup will taste especially
sweet, as it soothes the memory

of all that hustling.

Children's Psychiatric Hospital

"I got bit by a Rottweiler, but I still love
dogs," she says, pointing to her forehead. "Like,
130 stitches. When I was four."

In her room, observing what she presents
on the other side of the bed, the hope in her Jesus
cutout, the girly things of age fourteen. "So, Thalia,"
I begin, "what is up with this *thing* that happened
yesterday? Running into traffic?"

She smiles, pulling her long brown hair back. "There
wasn't any *traffic*," she protests. "It was just
an empty street."

I take notes on a makeshift desk, in my suit, trying
not to be the white man. "Are you really in a gang?"
I continue, softening here with authentic curiosity.
"I mean," looking into her green eyes &
received with the dim vacancy of what is being
formed, "you are so young. What do they call
you in here? *Teddy Bear*?"

She pauses to collect her thoughts.

"It's no big deal, really. My friends, my cousins . . .
they just ask you to join."

The white cinderblock of her room holds these
memories, a history of commotion & suspension &
the overall baffling presence in here of these young
girls.

"And the incident a couple of weeks back?" my
inquisition continues. "Where does *that* come from?"

32

Thalia is enjoying this conversation immensely, if
nothing else because of the sound of her isolation.

"She hit me first," she answers without apology. "Then
there was all of this blood," she adds shyly. "I guess
I hit her in the wrong place."

I start to gather my files. "Well," I reply, "I certainly
wouldn't mess with you, *Teddy Bear*."

We both laugh.

Let us dance around the pagan fire, celebrating
the pointed stick, the kerosene of what lives
underneath our lives.

Gerzon

Another one, all of fourteen, quickly explaining
the secret of his spotless behavior so far: "Because
I don't want to bangggkk. I'm not down no more."

This is the boys' psych unit, always surprising
in its relative tranquility, & what can be explained
at least partially by the wizardry of chemical
combinations.

"It's safer in here," Gerzon continues, & goes on
to explain how it hurt when he saw his father buy
the neighbor kid a brand-new bike at Walmart. "It's
the family he's with now," he clarifies quietly.
"It just set me off . . ."

Gerzon's burglaries, the loot of thievery: a Fender
Stratocaster, a propane heater, a Black & Decker saw.

"I don't know what was going on then . . ." his shoulders
sag. "But next time, maybe I'll do better on the
outs? I won't have to earn my dots no more—"

Which is why we are here, I interject, doubling
down on protocol. A plan, so that you will not have
to come back to a place like this,

crafted by well-meaning professionals.

A hopeful push maybe, into the head wind that informs
your life? Some kind of lucky costume that will keep
the darker energies at bay?

Twelve Hours in the Car

"Let's light fires!" she exclaims, my co-pilot
there in her front seat agony, with the multiple
lesions in her brain.

We are coasting down the interstate, high above the salt valley.

"She's like Miss Paris, 1985," she adds from out of
nowhere, our dog panting in the back seat. Below we can
see the triumphant freight trains that I once glided upon,

the outskirts of the Wyoming State Fair.
Blue sky, the occasional hawk, silence.

"But we wouldn't *wear* the moccasins," she continues, as
we concoct our resurrected future together: a hilltop
stone house, one story, carpet everywhere, & a bathroom
of soft rubber.

Maybe then I could maintain that the canyon never did make
me crazy? *This* time I would not invent a reason to
visit town—variations of thirst—and from our imaginary
living room we could see the 1920s.
Down below the massive town pool with its swirling
currents & bighorn rock construction.

All of this we could do, if we imagine it, as long as
the *other* dark presence cooperates. No longer
doomed, something else now, transformed in
her freckled smile,

the first one for miles.

Our Las Cruces Hearings

It is indeed a private jet, & I match the women
with their shoes as they disembark, my
state-appointed board. The absence of security
at this small airport—here you can wait, literally,
on the runway—amid the festive tin tables &
conversation of old pilots. Miniature planes
suspended from the beams, the talent of appreciation
in all of its innocence.

But off we go to the facility, which happens to be
less than three-hundred yards away, & once again
we are in the visceral and unsubtle stories that await us,
by now merging into their one universal theme of deprivation.

On this day, however, an almost vacation air because
we actually have a window—outside the desert
landscape, an occasional roadrunner—as the succession
commences:

Grandfather Garcia from Roswell with his, "he'll be in
my house now," the list of rules on his refrigerator.

The studious fifteen-year-old named from a Russian
baby book & how he wants the boot camp now
more than anything, the roamings of a Carlsbad gang
nowhere close to where he intends to be.

And then the tall, muscular legitimate athlete, his 4.4
time ready to be placed in front of any college's
self-interest, & how most of what Denvis has known
so far is home invasion and parents addicted to crack.

And finally, the kid nobody likes but me, with
his photographic memory gone to paint but his flaring
will is what *might* carry him through the streets of
Hobbs in a less uncertain manner.

These have become my kids, their destiny is my
diagnosis & in their reflection is an endless succession
of teachings about what we are all brought into,

so thoroughly in its salting.

A Visitation From Sister Sue

In my nun's Irish green eyes I see the reflection of
service, of being alone & conspicuous.

"Why is it," I begin in my dream, "that some of us
so readily follow the solitary orbit? You have your
nun's habit, and your similarly diminished station. I
have nothing but what the years of aspiration
sculpted, sustained by the present tense
that now seems so remote—"

"Are you asking me a question?" Sister Sue interrupts.

"Yes," I reply. "And in seeing you I feel the prospect
of an answer . . . Why is this so *easy*?"

"We are impossibly earnest, both of us, it is
true," she replies. "But also bound to the notion
of what can never be achieved." She hesitates, then
continues, "There is only the statement of our
odd lives that we can fully celebrate each
incandescent afternoon."

This unique & important way of dying.

Life Presents Difficult Choices

I will choose the House of Mourning instead
of the House of Joy any day.

Without her building grimace I would have no compass.
Only the impulse of my need.

Still, she moves away from my touch.

Will I always have this mask?

Suspended from Summer Prep School

All I ever got from that place was the
desire to steal, as in what we staged in
the depth of July, irresistible all of those
uniforms, jerseys & warm-ups
in the padlocked storage room.

We hid our loot in a pillow case way up
in the ventilation ducts of the brand-new
Choate Arts Center.

Thus I became a file,
like the ones I preside over now.

Actions symbolic of the deep emotional
stamp, our underpinnings, or the way
the world works on you, early on,

relentlessly

insisting upon a response.

Poetry at the Juvie

(for Jimmy Santiago Baca)

"The pain in the streets is what I want to talk
about," Rosita says. She then hangs on
his response, the shock of being personally visited by
him,
here at the juvenile detention center.

"Read for me," he says to Rosita firmly, injecting
the dignity of his craft into our lockup.

Rosita responds, from her floral-patterned journal,
nervous but wanting
someone
to listen, as her own spoken beauty informs the room,
risking even a reference to the standard violation
from a masculine presence, & having read her
file I know the details.

Our juvie girls are *so* pretty, *so* much
the target of a seamy world framed by
the opportunity in bad centuries.

She alludes to this pain in the streets and by so doing
it proves Jimmy's point that such expression is universal,
that the Anglo world so impersonal can suddenly shift
with a few words in the right key,
phrases that hit home like an injury
to one of their own.

We remain in the trance of Rosita speaking of her regretful
acts, as one more sweet voice begins to find itself.

Alone now, she is dialed into the triumph of her own life.

Mary Oliver's Limitations

I try to believe that I am a part of some remote
but important flock, as she has promised, in
the high blue air, united by the choices that we
make, & the progression of their

consequence.

The years that take you out . . .

gone, in that kind of blue.

Fourth of July in New Mexico

Father, stepmother, stepsister, in the time it
takes for a first sip of morning coffee, the finality
of his aim. And then, being a rancher's kid, the
logical choice of a bulldozer with which to bury them,
knowing
as he does where the keys are.

The manure bin will do.

How the whole point is to show up liberated
at his girlfriend's house, in his dad's pickup,
oddly restrained in his jubilation.

"Dang, how did you manage this?" his sweetheart
asks, regarding the green Ford pickup.

"It is different now," he says cryptically. "But
would you still like me either way? If I had done
something bad?"

She smiles, unsure of his meaning, before
the helicopters & news outlets arrive, intruding
upon his longed-for normal weekend—July Fourth no less.

A blowtorch was his punishment the night before.
And yet here he is with his Juliet of the eastern
New Mexico plains, still reluctant to shed his
buttoned-up cowboy shirt,
despite the bong hits & improvised basketball
before the audience of her friends and
her soulful brown eyes.

This is how it goes out here, in this vast expanse of
cruelty & rancher's jokes. What a weekend he had, though,
just hanging with Denicia and classmates, not hearing the
rumors starting to build, & evening news to follow. No
longer enduring his father's ridicule, his taunting, the daily
punishment culminating in the bizarre sexual
invitation, Colter's refusal, then the blowtorch.

All of us can be pushed too far, and recourse is
what adolescence is.

Now he can drive the truck.

Now he can join his seven-boy team for August two-a-days.

Now he can ride the fence line.

Now he can begin to process what was done to him.

Thinking of Her

Eleven precise steps to the kitchen, balancing
the yogurt & hypodermic needle filled with
some alternative vitamin potion—hopeful,
symbolic, she can walk but not without the
perilous tilting & I can abide these bruises no
longer, the yellowish hue of our love . . . Brutish,
surreal, not exactly happy, but no joking
eternal or whatever it is that comes to you in
these moments, deep in the night, alone in bed

fearing what the pain is bringing in.

Kirsten

Wind through her teen curls, as if *sir*
could transform her world? Where a question
is asked, & silence ensues?
She will do anything for her freedom, which means
that she will keep calling me
who represents the state in this matter.

"My hands are tied," I tell her. "But let's see if we
can be creative? At least you are calling,
instead of just running—"

And what is it that you are running to? Remnants
of a broken camp, the canvas tent all packed up?
Or your home, where your enthusiasm is met
by the muting of a remote?

The sweet amnesia of the present tense, the sugar
of what can be blocked out, or forgotten?

I try to be reassuring in my next daily call: "Hi there.
This is your new friend, the guy from the Juvenile
Authority . . ."

As we go over who she is
versus her desire to be gone
from the semi-locked facility. As with all
of these children our barter
is in the trading of months & weeks: "Make
it September 21 and you can final on October
20? Deal?"

Appointed by the governor, I am now allowed
to exchange time for good deeds.
Of course Kirsten is "Casper" in several different
gangs—the little white girl at the mercy of her passion
for flight.

She is a *runner*.

It is what she knows. And she can assess
the opportunity in an instant; when the urge comes
over her, it becomes her being & it is to the highway
she goes, where Joey her boy will always pick her up.

So just like that she is off again, flying
to the promise of the next moment. Forgetful

in the sweet wind, her dangerous thumb extended
on the midmorning highway,

remembering what she never had.

Isais

Isais says: "I have always had a dream of being on
one of those cruiser boats."

We ask him how things are at home.

"Nothing really good," he replies.

And finally, before the hearing ends, he pitches
his own redemption: "I found out that
I could bring my own brain cells back," he says.
"For reals."

Then he picks up his neatly prepared notebook,
hopeful into the lobby he goes as we make our
decision to throw him to the wolves.

Snakes

Meanwhile, the other kid, with his engaging
accent & reptile collection. He is similarly
pursuing the resurrection of a more simplified
kind—very earthbound, revolving around
an equation of need.

He kind of looks like a reptile himself, his gang
name is Cueball, & he likes the idea of a high-
altitude reintegration center, with its logging work.

Fourteen an hour.

"Nothing but flannel," he says.

Bartlett Mesa

(for Aunt Nanette Bartlett)

"Sir, I don't mean it's a *bad* mesa . . ."

Of course you don't. I was young once. Bad
means good, duh.

The boy continues: "From that mesa you can see
the whole valley. There's a lake up there too—"

I want to tell him how my great aunt once-removed
surmised this splendid, over-the-top demesne
with its streams and mountains and
alarming closest town.

Back to Chicago, she insisted.
1919, despite the stone mansion and attentive staff.
She crossed Raton Pass too—as Alejandro soon would—
his future an uncertain turn
unlike what awaited her in cushioned Winnetka, leaving
those mining families to their own choices.

But Alejandro will start over with his mother, and
this time it will be different. In anonymous Colorado,
he will do well,
until he meets his first real friend.

Our Second Trip to Montana

I. Crow Reservation

Miles back, a plump falcon on the ranch fence, measuring
the distance between the car and what is insanely
possible.

Her face suddenly reddens, heats up like a crack
pipe, as she starts to twitch. "I am hot," she says
excitedly. "I can't take this. . . ."

We are stuck between Lodge Grass and Sheridan, no
exits or trees or hint of shade—as such this circumstance
symbolizes our very alliance.

The Volvo air conditioner continues to fade out
along with our hope for something else.

'There is an exit coming up soon," I say with
concocted assurance. The rolling headlands of this
permutation of prairie,
the distant blue mountains,
the memory of Custer's sun-ravaged men everywhere
as her temperature skyrockets before my very eyes,
the sun going straight to her brain
because of the lesions.

I have vowed not to speak of this anymore.

But . . . our hope is affirmed as the air suddenly blows
cold like a promise fulfilled.

I am silent because . . . what would *you* do if said pain
had you under its boot? Never really going away and
mocking your own faith? What if *you* were strapped in
with a brooding and resentful presence like me?

II. A New Mall

Or, how about this? Pulling up to the mall just off 1-25
north of Denver, seeking the blue parking space & a short
walk to Starbucks. . . . No luck. Distance is their message.

Trying again in the heat to similarly gain access to the
popular Chinese bistro, by now livid I am with the teenage
hostesses clustered in their home behind the counter.
"How do you expect us to eat in here?" I begin. "You
have to walk a mile just to get to your doorway. . . . And
we are supposed to embarrass ourselves in front of *that*
throng?" I say, pointing to the jammed dining
room with its barn full of activity and no empty tables,
the oversized room with its single eye.

The girls are speechless, maybe frightened.

(I am better than this . . .)

"Is it okay if we use the side door?" I continue, a little
calmer. They quickly nod yes,
patrolling the afternoon in their comfort.

III. Books on Tape

And finally, peacefully cruising—this time in air-
conditioned bliss, under the impression that she has
been lulled into sleep by the iambic rhythms of Fitzgerald
on tape, until she suddenly sits up in her passenger seat.
"Why won't this thing move backwards," she says angrily,
slamming the seat with her fist. "It

won't move . . . I feel trapped—" "Okay, okay . . ."
I reply with soft assurance, slowing down to the
shoulder of nowhere. "I can't *breathe*," she continues.
"The sun is just blasting me up here . . ."

Everything is handled, not calmly, as the back seat proves to
be the merciful solution.

I cannot leave this circumstance.

Why would I?

After Work

There on the restaurant patio, where my doomed
longings transpired as if I were invisible to myself.

Dizzy with phone numbers, but always the reasons
for delay. Or in the surprise caress of my hair
from a blonde stranger named *Bunny*.

Or that educated trio of attractive female
attorneys, commenting upon my elusive presence.

"What do you *mean*?" I protest.

"You are always alone with your paper," the women continue.

Always protecting
what I cannot remember.

The Untimely Death of a Panhandler

She's barely thirty—freckled, meth-thin,
with her devoted transient partner, a big guy
in a T-shirt. She is dead now, apparently run
over by a swerving car—according to the newspaper—no
more begging in the two-o'clock oven.

But she was *so* pretty, I could tell from my car in
the after-work drive: petite, red-haired, floating
above her own unfortunate circumstance.

It has been established that when you cry
you cry for yourself, and in this case
it is no different: if I could have held her but
once, urged her toward whatever she defined
as a better place, then maybe I could forget
my own years of Thai stick, Jack Daniels, my
own embarrassment of privilege.

But that guy loved her, I could tell that too. With
his Confederate cap. He would hold her so
delicately as the light turned to green, it being
after work for most of us & the urgency of getting home.

Leaving the dusty couple to their night's challenge.

Hope House Denied:
Unwelcome in Santa Fe

Deadlines and signatures and the buzz-
killer of a neighborhood's hate.

What manifests at the monthly association
meeting, where what is to be protected
confirms the definition of empty.

They fight because what we all possess
on this earth is actually so . . .

It is resolved that there will be no ex-cons next door.

Self-satisfied, they drive home
into their resplendent night.

Montana, Again

Meanwhile, to violate my previously stated
oath, how can I lay off what the yellow dashboard
light evokes?

I will contain our peril in my distracted silence, as the highway
between Cuba and Farmington is a desolate one, and as
I will believe anything spoken by a confident mechanic.
The promise is inside of our station wagon—our private
world rolling now through the long rhythms
between towns, as once again the dog needs water.

If alone, I would drive straight through to whatever
distant planet now frames the center of my leisure,
fingers tight on the wheel, with this same commitment
to ignoring pain.

It is Farmington now in its raw form—the very slow Dairy
Queen line, a shirtless man, his arms covered with gauze,
while outside she is overheating, along with my car.

Later, to switch the mood I talk politics, but
it reverts back to her mother's malevolent ways: the way
she burned her doll and then vanished upstairs for
months. Farmwork, and the story of catching a man.
The memory of our Shiprock rest stop, giving
way to the jumpiness of a rural gas station just over
the Colorado line: tattoos, meth, working the buzz
as everything is elsewhere.

Through Canyon Lands in twilight, the shadows
predicting the future in their defined shape, the Flintstone
formations. Then, finally, we make the southern edge
of Moab and the new motel where they have never heard
of a handicapped person, or of requests involving
the concept of proximity.

But really, if time *is* running out on us,
it would be so like this, but not necessarily in proper order:
the electrode grips of yet another quack doctor, this
time in Montana. Or how they welcomed her as their
own lost daughter there on my arm, an unspoken
celebration of her presence in their lives.

And then, purchasing fine, fuzzy deer at the tourist
shop, her concern about our dog upstaging the freight
trains that no longer appear, her former boss at the vintage
shop looking at her with shock:

"What *happened* to you?"

she asks with railroad-town honesty.

Then, imagining a perfect world in the distance between
Livingston and Billings, the yellow light no longer on. We savor
the indignity of hope, the clarity in a simple task survived—
gradually dancing its blessing, the triumph of our witness.

Breakfast with My Patron

I drink to my own mortality each morning,
in salutation to the choreography that I can never
truly join in:

the noted & astute professional company that
clearly efforts to quantify what does not exist.

As pointless as what passes for a life.

Years in the mineshaft of state government, yet
buoyed by this sunlit breakfast conversation as we map
out the coming weeks.

"He might not be finished with you," he says, half-
teasing, half-menacing, invoking our governor.

Political topics,
always there for the men to discuss.

Policy Meetings

Conspicuous in my meeting voice,
attempting to blend in while the dull &
predictable assemblage rises with: "That's
precisely the box we need to think outside
of . . ."

Or, "It is *mission critical* that we roll this out
before the cessation of the fiscal year . . ."

Always wincing at what I hear myself saying,
the assumptions that others make about my visage.

God gives us amnesia. Then says, *good luck.*

Central Avenue

Matching Hoppity as we survey Central Avenue one
half hour before noon,
the same broken families with their helpless
progeny finding the home of their street.

Hippity explains it to me, waving his hands as
he does; together we walk down the forlorn
avenue: motels, the cheap assessment of a day, or
what can be done amid Spandex & where appetites
reach their logical conclusion.

"Why bother?" I ask rhetorically: "The same people,
this endless stream that I see in the mirror of
my Volvo? People like us must need to feel
viable, I guess . . ."

And Hoppity, characteristically misunderstanding:
"No!" he exclaims. "That isn't true. It *does* make
a difference. Just ask our Hope House alumni—"

I could say a number of things at this point:

"Is Sam still on the avenue gunning his stolen
dump truck?"

"Is the whole point simply to not bounce checks?"

"To be normal enough to safely navigate the mall?"

Or, "The avenue waits here every day for what washes
in, the dry air of our longing."

Or, "What would my life have been without
this need to *improve* the surrounding world?"

But I say nothing.

"See?" Hippity continues in his not getting. "It
is undeniable. We *can* improve our lot!"

Okay. But it will always be there, as a man
slows down and detours around the block,
need that drives our being; she awaits on the street . . .

Or the cavernous movie theaters jammed, without
surprise, everything becoming

way too simple,

the beaming couples holding their newborns like collateral.

The Fifties Are Back

She pulls me aside, having
watched me over the years. "You
and I are similar," she says. "We are
both way too comfortable in where we don't
belong."

Finally, putting to rest the bad idea
of rebellious circumstance. Welcome to
the fifties instead, their furious resurrection
everywhere to be found, this devotion to
running downhill—and why not?

Anything else is aberration. Console
yourself as best you can with pure black
coffee and sports radio.

The measure is how you get on. No one
disputes this.

Look around you in this very restaurant. . . . Why
complicate things when the barista's eyes
are so green? And what is it that you want to
know anyway? Truth is in the numbers.

Try talking to the earth instead, kneeling
in body prayer, & do not come at me with your
sullen, less-than-perfect life.

This is what we do here.

Political Aspirations

So perhaps I will once again walk the neighborhoods &
seek special meaning in the duty of service.

"I do not know that agency, but will inquire
on your behalf," I will say.

Voter courtship, the spring primary season, out
on the different shades of asphalt, new
homes in all of their suburban glory,
in what can be measured.

Yet always back to the two of us.

I do promise that we will move north someday,
if I ever lose another election, & you can swim
in that Olympian pool. Wyoming,
so retro in its use of actual boulders,
its shimmering depth & unlikely currents

to be spotted from twenty-thousand feet above.

Cowgirl Bar

Awkward in the crowded bar, and yet
the swift flash of eyes that Whitman spoke about,
promising love.

It is not her fault rather mine as I navigate
the packed saloon; the band is good with the
curvy singer & her kids in knit caps backing her up.
She plays the mandolin & I am trying to remember
that line of ancient Persian kings.

Then, impulsive conversation, recounting my sputtering
endorsement interview & the legislative day's high point
as the old Navajo senator shed his blanket and cast
his dramatic vote, then
the potato song as his encore.

Xerxes, Cyrus, Darius . . .

Across the wooden floor she sits high on the chair,
maneuvering her amiable legs, & we both know
that we are sisters never to touch.

Inauguration Night

The governor again. "Good luck, guy,"
I say, smiling with him into the camera, his
arm around me. "I am thinking of you,"
he answers. "The people like you. You are
with me as I do this."

When he says thanks this time he really means
it, as if a revelation or new poll has sobered
his bunch.

No refuge from the demeaning I concocted
my own route, which always worked
so much better in this primitive world of
attraction.

I *filter*.

Nevertheless, I am buzzed on the elusive
bodies of others,

her smile pure erasure.